KU-473-322

First published in Great Britain
in 2013

This edition 2021

Designed and typeset by
Something More Creative®

10Publishing, a division of
10ofthose.com
Unit C, Tomlinson Road, Leyland,
PR25 2DY, England
Email: info@10ofthose.com
Website: www.10ofthose.com

ISBN: 978-1-913896-33-1
Printed in the United Kingdom

1 3 5 7 10 8 6 4 2

BOOK 1

The Word

one to one

Journey through John's Gospel with a friend

The Word One to One helps you get started with the Bible.

How it works

On the left is text from 'John's Gospel' – one of the books of the Bible:

- John lived with Jesus for three action packed years.

- We'll read the account of what he saw and heard during that time.

On the right are notes to chat through with a friend:

- They highlight the main points from John's Gospel and provide background information from the rest of the Bible.
- Many have found that talking these through with a Christian friend – one to one or in a small group – has been a great introduction to the historical person Jesus.

Episode 1

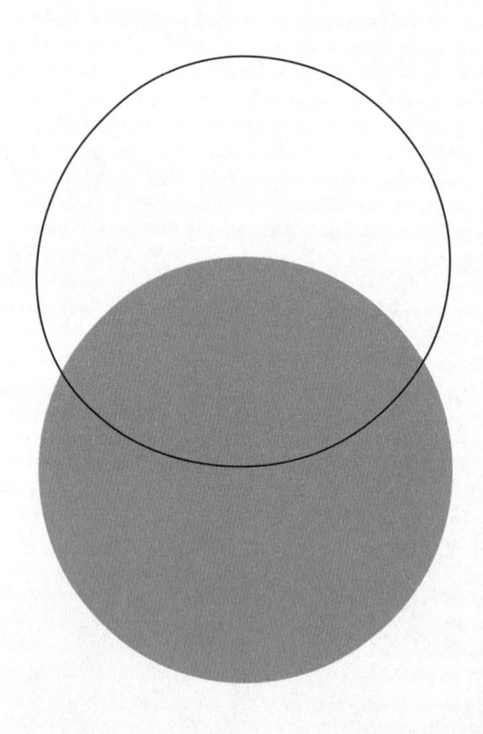

God came to earth

JOHN 1:1–18

In this episode:
John's eyewitness account starts with an overview.

You might find this a surprising start. We don't begin with the baby Jesus and His famous birth.

There is no stable, no angels, no Bethlehem... but rather some massive claims... so don't be surprised if it will need some unpacking.

This is what John wrote – read this first

[1] In the beginning was the Word, and the Word was with God, and the Word was God.

[2] He was with God in the beginning.

[3] Through him all things were made; without him nothing was made that has been made.

Then use the notes to chat it through

The God who made everything

John introduces us to 'the Word':

- Twice he says the Word was there 'in the beginning.'
- So the Word existed before time, before creation, before the beginning...
- In short... the Word is eternal.

But who or what is the Word?

- The Word is God. **(v. 1)**
- The Word is a person, see how the sentence starts with 'He.' **(v. 2)**
- The Word, who is God and a person, made absolutely everything, no exceptions. **(v. 3)**

Already we're being introduced to the Creator!

But John's claims for the Word go even further...

[4] In him was life, and that life was the light of all mankind.

[5] The light shines in the darkness, and the darkness has not overcome it.

But what difference does the Word make for life?

- As Creator, the Word is the source of physical life. **(v. 4)**
- But as we'll see, He is also the source of eternal life.
- The Word gives understanding for life (light). **(v. 4)**
- The darkness in our world can't stop Him bringing life and light to mankind. **(v. 5)**

For 2,000 years His life-giving message has been going out unchanged.

There are more believers around the world today than ever before.

In fact...

The light of the Word continues to shine today.

[6] There was a man sent from God whose name was John.

[7] He came as a witness to testify concerning that light, so that through him all might believe.

[8] He himself was not the light; he came only as a witness to the light.

[9] The true light that gives light to everyone was coming into the world.

The life He offers

John (the writer) now introduces John the Baptist. We'll see later that he was the sensation of his day – drawing huge crowds to the desert with his preaching.

Just look at his job description:

- God Himself appointed him. (v. 6)
- He testifies – like a witness in a court... (v. 7)
- ...preparing people for the Word, now called the light... (v. 8)
- ...who was soon to come into the world. (v. 9)

John the Baptist is the warm-up act. Through him God makes sure that the arrival of the Word is publicly known.

We still haven't been told who the Word is...

[10] He was in the world, and though the world was made through him, the world did not recognise him.

[11] He came to that which was his own, but his own did not receive him.

[12] Yet to all who did receive him, to those who believed in his name, he gave the right to become children of God –

What was the response when the 'light' came?

- The world did not recognise its Creator. **(v. 10)**
- Born a Jew, even His own people rejected Him. **(v. 11)**

But look at this mind-blowing gift for those who accepted Him:

- He adopted them into God's own family! **(v. 12)**
- They were given the full privileges of being a child of God for ever! **(v. 12)**

Imagine a helpless orphan adopted into the wealthiest, most influential family on the planet... God's gift is way bigger even than that.

[13] children born not of natural descent, nor of human decision or a husband's will, but born of God.

Who gets this extraordinary gift?

- Not people born into a religious family (natural descent).
- Not people who somehow became religious (human decision).
- But people adopted (born) into God's family.

What is on offer through the Word is a new life. A living relationship with God for ever as a loving Father.

[14] The Word became flesh and made his dwelling among us.

We have seen his glory, the glory of the one and only Son, who came from the Father, full of grace and truth.

[15] (John testified concerning him. He cried out, saying, 'This is the one I spoke about when I said, "He who comes after me has surpassed me because he was before me."')

Grace: God's undeserved kindness and love, freely given.

Truth: the answer to all our searching.

God shows Himself on earth

Here is the crucial claim:
God became human and moved into the neighbourhood! **(v. 14)**

What evidence is given to back this up?

- John (the writer) was one of many who saw the Word first-hand. **(v. 14)**
- John and his friends saw Him come not in a whirlwind of power and might but full of grace and truth. **(v. 14)**
- They came to the conclusion that He is God's Son here on earth! **(v. 14)**
- We also have the public and powerful witness of John the Baptist who says the person he will introduce is his Creator. **(v. 15)**

These witnesses are saying that the Creator came to live on earth at a specific time, in a specific place. They are saying that they were there when He came, and they want to tell us about Him.

So it's God's Son but what is His name?

[16] Out of his fullness we have all received grace in place of grace already given.

[17] For the law was given through Moses; grace and truth came through Jesus Christ.

[18] No one has ever seen God, but the one and only Son, who is himself God and is in the closest relationship with the Father, has made him known.

Moses: the greatest Old Testament prophet (around 1300 BC). God gave His law to the Israelites through him.

Look at what John (the writer) tells us:

- The Son is overflowing with grace. (v. 16)
- God's good law, given through Moses long ago, is now to be fulfilled in Jesus. (v. 17)
- The Word is God's eternal Son – Jesus Christ. (v. 17)
- He makes God known today. (v. 18)

At last John tells us: Jesus Christ is the Word, the Creator, the eternal Son of God, who makes His Father known today.

He does not burden life with rules – instead, He brings grace and truth.

Summary

What have we seen about Jesus, the Word, so far?

- He was there before the world existed. (v. 1)
- He is God. (v. 1)
- He made everything. (v. 3)
- He has life in Himself and brings light to all people. (v. 4)
- Those who believe in Him become members of God's own family. (v. 12)
- The Word came to earth as a man. (v. 14)
- He doesn't bring rules but grace and truth. (v. 17)
- John claims that we can know God personally through Jesus Christ. (v. 18)

How does this introduction compare with what you had thought of Jesus Christ?

[1] In the beginning was the Word… and the Word was God.

[3] Through him all things were made…

[4] In him was life and that life was the light of all mankind.

[12] …to all who did receive him, to those who believed in his name, he gave the right to become children of God…

[14] The Word became flesh and made his dwelling among us.

[17] …grace and truth came through Jesus Christ.

[18] No one has ever seen God, but the one and only Son… has made him known.

Why not find a moment to re-read what we've looked at in this episode?

John 1:1–18

[1] In the beginning was the Word, and the Word was with God, and the Word was God. [2] He was with God in the beginning. [3] Through him all things were made; without him nothing was made that has been made. [4] In him was life, and that life was the light of all mankind. [5] The light shines in the darkness, and the darkness has not overcome it. [6] There was a man sent from God whose name was John. [7] He came as a witness to testify concerning that light, so that through him all might believe. [8] He himself was not the light; he came only as a witness to the light.

[9] The true light that gives light to everyone was coming into the world. [10] He was in the world, and though the world was made through him, the world did not recognise him. [11] He came to that which was his own, but his own did not receive him. [12] Yet to all who did receive him, to those who believed in his name, he gave the right to become children of God – [13] children born not of natural descent, nor of human decision or a husband's will, but born of God. [14] The Word became flesh and made his dwelling among us. We have seen his glory, the glory of the one and only Son, who came from the Father, full of grace and truth. [15] (John testified concerning him. He cried out, saying, 'This is the one I spoke about when I said, "He who comes after me has surpassed me because he was before me."') [16] Out of his fullness we have all received grace in place of grace already given. [17] For the law was given through Moses; grace and truth came through Jesus Christ. [18] No one has ever seen God, but the one and only Son, who is himself God and is in the closest relationship with the Father, has made him known.

What comes next?
We'll see John the Baptist, the warm-up act, before Jesus comes onto the scene.

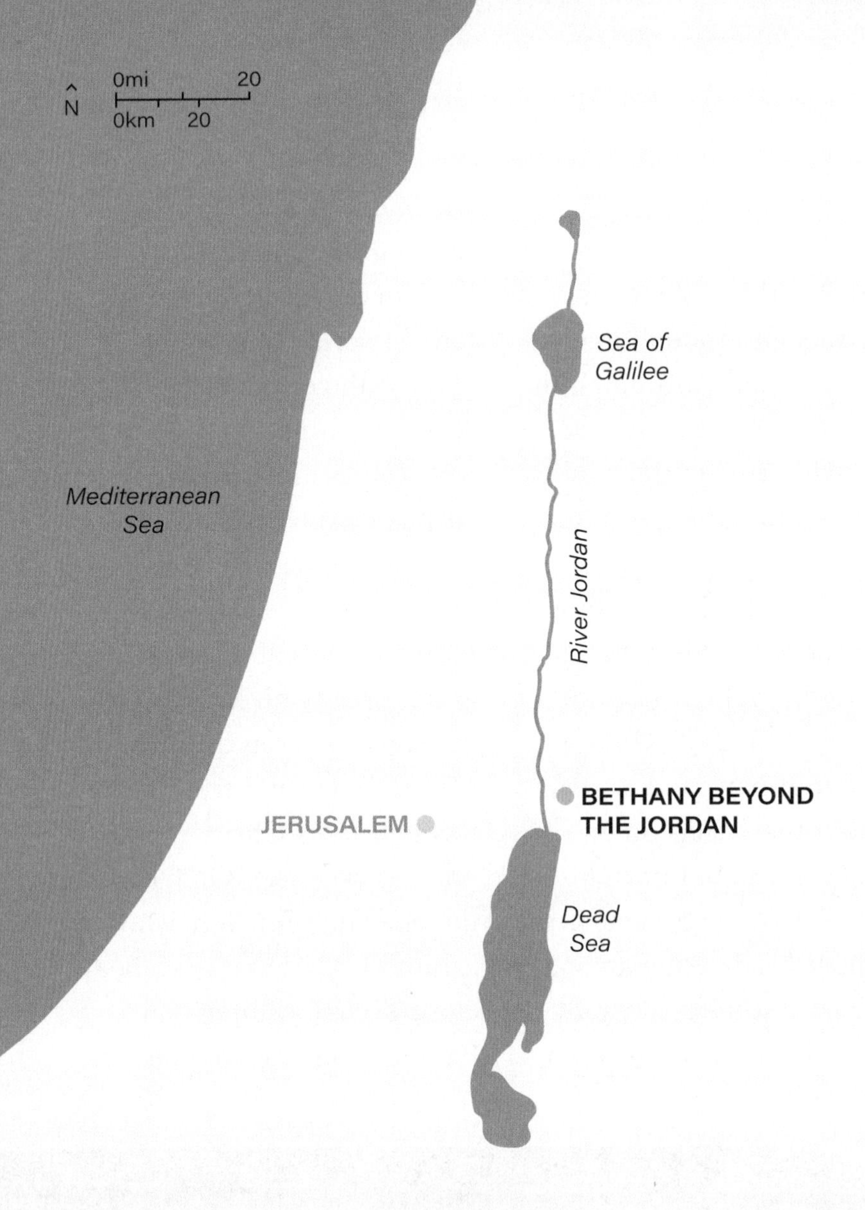
N
0mi
20
0km
20
Sea of
Galilee
Mediterranean
Sea
River Jordan
BETHANY BEYOND
THE JORDAN
JERUSALEM
Dead
Sea

Episode 2

The warm-up act

JOHN 1:19–34

In the previous episode: John introduces Jesus Christ as God come to earth.

In this episode: John the Baptist prepares the way for the dramatic arrival of Jesus.

[19] Now this was John's testimony when the Jewish leaders in Jerusalem sent priests and Levites to ask him who he was.

[20] He did not fail to confess, but confessed freely, 'I am not the Messiah.'

[21] They asked him, 'Then who are you? Are you Elijah?' He said, 'I am not.' 'Are you the Prophet?' He answered, 'No.'

[22] Finally they said, 'Who are you? Give us an answer to take back to those who sent us. What do you say about yourself?'

Levites: priests from the Israelite tribe of Levi.

Messiah: God's chosen King, the promised Saviour who would rescue Israel and the world.

Elijah: a famous Israelite prophet (around 860 BC) – Israel was expecting his return.

John the Baptist arrives... but why?

John the Baptist was the top item on the news. Today, TV cameras, reporters and social media would be broadcasting his every word.

The Jewish leaders have been watching for signs of the Messiah they had been promised – understandably they wonder if John is the man.

They send religious leaders to quiz John. **(v. 19)**

How does the religious leaders' questioning turn out? Not well! John's testimony is clear:

- 'I am not the Messiah.' **(v. 20)**
- 'Are you Elijah?' No. **(v. 21)**
- 'Are you the Prophet.' No. **(v. 21)**
- 'Who are you then? We need something to say to the people who sent us!' **(v. 22)**

John doesn't want to be the centre of attention. He is not the Messiah.

The Prophet: God had promised that He would send another prophet like Moses to lead His people.

So who is John and what is he all about?

[23] John replied in the words of Isaiah the prophet, 'I am the voice of one calling in the wilderness, "Make straight the way for the Lord."'

Get ready...

Isaiah was another great prophet sent by God (around 700 BC). He spoke about what would happen when the Messiah came. John the Baptist uses words from Isaiah's book to describe his own job.

Isaiah 40:3 tells of exactly this moment:
'Prepare the way for the Lord...
a highway for our God.'

In the days of great empires, it was normal practice to create wide highways as entrances to major cities, so that a victorious leader could parade, or triumph, in front of his people.

What is John the Baptist telling them?

- He is urging the people to get ready...

God Himself is coming!

[24] Now the Pharisees who had been sent [25] questioned him, 'Why then do you baptise if you are not the Messiah, nor Elijah, nor the Prophet?'

[26] 'I baptise with water,' John replied, 'but among you stands one you do not know.

[27] He is the one who comes after me, the straps of whose sandals I am not worthy to untie.'

[28] This all happened at Bethany on the other side of the Jordan, where John was baptising.

It's not me you're looking for...

Again John is questioned, again he points forwards:

- He could only wash with water. (v. 26)
- But One far greater is on His way! (v. 27)

Back in a time of open sandals, in hot dusty streets full of animals, washing feet was a job for the lowest servant in your house.

Jesus is such a big deal that John the Baptist says he is not even worthy to untie His sandals, let alone wash His feet!

We are regularly given historically accurate details as if to say, 'Go check and see if what I am saying is correct.' (v. 28)

Pharisees: mostly local officials, who were very religious and well-respected.

Baptise: to wash (or dunk) in water. People were baptised to publicly show they wanted to turn back to God.

[29] The next day John saw Jesus coming towards him and said, 'Look, the Lamb of God, who takes away the sin of the world!

[30] This is the one I meant when I said, "A man who comes after me has surpassed me because he was before me."

[31] I myself did not know him, but the reason I came baptising with water was that he might be revealed to Israel.'

Passover: remembers God rescuing His people from slavery in Egypt around 1300 BC. Pharaoh had set himself against God and His people, enslaving them and murdering their sons. Despite many warnings Pharaoh refused to change his ways.

On Passover night the angel of death passed through Egypt and killed every firstborn son as God acted in judgement. There was only one escape: the Jews were to put the blood of a spotless lamb on their doorposts. This was a lamb that had lived with the family for four days, a lamb that then died in the place of the firstborn son. Where the blood was, a death had already taken place, and the judgement passed over.

The Lamb of God

And then, the moment we've been waiting for, John sees Jesus:

- He shouts out this unique title: 'the Lamb of God'! (v. 29)
- He explains that Jesus was around before John was born. (v. 30) (Of course He was – He is our Creator, remember Episode 1?)
- John's job was to prepare people for the arrival of Jesus... (v. 31)

John can't help himself. The very first time he sees Jesus he shouts out:

'Look! See that man there? He has come from God to die. Why? To take away the sin of the world! That is His mission.'

This special title – Lamb of God – tells us straightaway what Jesus has come to do...

Jesus will die for the sin of the world to make us right with God.

This is an offer to all people everywhere, whoever we are. (v. 29)

[32] Then John gave this testimony: 'I saw the Spirit come down from heaven as a dove and remain on him.

[33] And I myself did not know him, but the one who sent me to baptise with water told me, "The man on whom you see the Spirit come down and remain is the one who will baptise with the Holy Spirit."

[34] I have seen and I testify that this is God's Chosen One.'

Holy Spirit: the Bible tells us that God is three in one. He is God the Father, God the Son (Jesus), and God the Holy Spirit.

The Spirit-filled King

Like a witness in a courtroom, John the Baptist says exactly what he saw:

- In Israel's past, the Holy Spirit frequently 'fell' on God's chosen kings, but just for a short time.
- This is different. John saw the Spirit come down on Jesus... and stay! **(v. 32)**

What will Jesus, God's Spirit-filled King, do?

- Jesus will fill people with God's Spirit – God's power and God's presence. No human being could do this. Only God can give Himself. **(v. 33)**

The Jews had been waiting since the first book of the Bible for these prophecies to be fulfilled.

John puts his neck on the line and says – Jesus is the One!

Summary

John the Baptist was all about getting people ready for Jesus. What has he taught us today?

- John the Baptist was a witness... (v. 19)
- ...a prophet preparing the way... (v. 23)
- ...but John was nothing compared to the One he introduced (remember the feet!). (v. 27)
- Jesus has come to die – He is uniquely the Lamb of God who takes away the sin of the world. (v. 29)
- Jesus is God's Spirit-filled Son. (v. 32)
- Jesus will flood us with God's presence (the Holy Spirit). (v. 33)
- John's testimony is clear – Jesus is the One! (v. 34)

What an introduction to Jesus! The time has arrived for the prophecies to be fulfilled. The Messiah has come.

19 Now this was John's
testimony...

23 'Make straight the
way for the Lord.'

27 '...whose sandals I am
not worthy to untie.'

29 '...the Lamb of God,
who takes away the sin
of the world!'

32 'I saw the Spirit come
down... and remain on him.'

33 "...the one who
will baptise with the
Holy Spirit."

34 '...this is God's
Chosen One.'

Why not find a moment to re-read what we've looked at in this episode?

John 1:19–34

[19] Now this was John's testimony when the Jewish leaders in Jerusalem sent priests and Levites to ask him who he was. [20] He did not fail to confess, but confessed freely, 'I am not the Messiah.' [21] They asked him, 'Then who are you? Are you Elijah?' He said, 'I am not.' 'Are you the Prophet?' He answered, 'No.' [22] Finally they said, 'Who are you? Give us an answer to take back to those who sent us. What do you say about yourself?' [23] John replied in the words of Isaiah the prophet, 'I am the voice of one calling in the wilderness, "Make straight the way for the Lord."'

[24] Now the Pharisees who had been sent [25] questioned him, 'Why then do you baptise if you are not the Messiah, nor Elijah, nor the Prophet?' [26] 'I baptise with water,' John replied, 'but among you stands one you do not know. [27] He is the one who comes after me, the straps of whose sandals I am not worthy to untie.' [28] This all happened at Bethany on the other side of the Jordan, where John was baptising. [29] The next day John saw Jesus coming towards him and said, 'Look, the Lamb of God, who takes away the sin of the world! [30] This is the one I meant when I said, "A man who comes after me has surpassed me because he was before me." [31] I myself did not know him, but the reason I came baptising with water was that he might be revealed to Israel.' [32] Then John gave this testimony: 'I saw the Spirit come down from heaven as a dove and remain on him. [33] And I myself did not know him, but the one who sent me to baptise with water told me, "The man on whom you see the Spirit come down and remain is the one who will baptise with the Holy Spirit." [34] I have seen and I testify that this is God's Chosen One.'

What comes next?
We're invited to
come and see Jesus.

Episode 3

Come and see!

JOHN 1:35-51

In the previous episode:
A mind-blowing claim...
Jesus is God on earth,
come to deal with what
keeps us from God.

In this episode:
Jesus arrives and
immediately attracts
followers.

[35] The next day John was there again with two of his disciples.

[36] When he saw Jesus passing by, he said, 'Look, the Lamb of God!'

[37] When the two disciples heard him say this, they followed Jesus.

Disciple: one who follows someone else and learns their way of life and teaching.

John the Baptist hands over

A day after his dramatic announcement about Jesus, John the Baptist is at it again.

He can't help himself 'Look, the Lamb of God!' **(v. 36)**

Immediately, two of John's followers (disciples) know they should be with Jesus.

It's Jesus' time now. John the Baptist's job is nearly done.

The timing is important. John (the writer) wants us to know that Jesus' disciples were eyewitnesses – they were there from the beginning of His public life.

[38] Turning round, Jesus saw them following and asked, 'What do you want?' They said, 'Rabbi' (which means 'Teacher'), 'where are you staying?'

[39] 'Come,' he replied, 'and you will see.' So they went and saw where he was staying, and they spent that day with him. It was about four in the afternoon.

Come and you'll see

Notice how the disciples immediately call Jesus 'Rabbi.' **(v. 38)**

What a life-changing day for these two men! They are called by Jesus and will be with Him from this moment on.

John wants us to know the eyewitness detail – even down to the time of day. **(v. 39)**

[40] Andrew, Simon Peter's brother, was one of the two who heard what John had said and who had followed Jesus.

[41] The first thing Andrew did was to find his brother Simon and tell him, 'We have found the Messiah' (that is, the Christ).

[42] And he brought him to Jesus.

Jesus looked at him and said, 'You are Simon son of John. You will be called Cephas' (which, when translated, is Peter).

Note that in verse 40 only one of the two is named. The other is John (the writer). We'll see throughout the book that although an eyewitness, his style is not to name himself.

After spending the day together, Jesus has made quite an impression on Andrew. The first thing he does is find his brother, Simon.

Andrew is so convinced he makes a huge claim – he's found the long-awaited Messiah.

Andrew brings his brother, Simon, who is renamed Cephas or Peter (the Aramaic word for rock).

Jesus will give him a foundational role in building every Christian community through his teaching.

[43] The next day Jesus decided to leave for Galilee. Finding Philip, he said to him, 'Follow me.'

[44] Philip, like Andrew and Peter, was from the town of Bethsaida.

[45] Philip found Nathanael and told him, 'We have found the one Moses wrote about in the Law, and about whom the prophets also wrote – Jesus of Nazareth, the son of Joseph.'

[46] 'Nazareth! Can anything good come from there?' Nathanael asked.

'Come and see,' said Philip.

Another encounter

Jesus finds Philip and there is no doubt in Philip's mind either... he too has met the Messiah.

But Nathanael needs convincing, with good reason.

What's behind Nathanael's scepticism?

- Nazareth is a northern town, full of different racial and religious groups. **(v. 45)**
- Because of the Jews' concern for religious purity, it was the last place they expected the Messiah to come from. **(v. 46)**

Just as Jesus says to the other two disciples back in verse 39, now Philip, with confidence, says, 'Come and see!'

[47] When Jesus saw Nathanael approaching, he said of him, 'Here truly is an Israelite in whom there is no deceit.'

[48] 'How do you know me?' Nathanael asked. Jesus answered, 'I saw you while you were still under the fig-tree before Philip called you.'

[49] Then Nathanael declared, 'Rabbi, you are the Son of God; you are the king of Israel.'

Jesus knows everything!

How is Nathanael convinced that Jesus is the Messiah?

- Jesus knows everything about Nathanael – there's no deceit in his heart. (v. 47)
- Incredibly, Jesus knows where he's been and what he's been doing, even though Jesus wasn't there to see. (v. 48)
- It's enough for Nathanael! He risks his reputation by shouting out who Jesus is. (v. 49)

Jesus is the Son of God, the King of Israel.

[50] Jesus said, 'You believe because I told you I saw you under the fig-tree. You will see greater things than that.'

[51] He then added, 'Very truly I tell you, you will see "heaven open, and the angels of God ascending and descending on" the Son of Man.'

Son of Man: is a title Jesus often gives Himself. It's from the Old Testament book of Daniel, written in about 600 BC. Daniel sees *'one like a son of man'* to whom God gives *'authority, glory and sovereign power; all nations and peoples of every language worshipped him.'* (Daniel 7:13–14)

Jesus is saying that He is this Son of Man.

What does Jesus promise?

- 'You haven't seen anything yet!' **(v. 50)**

Whenever Jesus starts a sentence with 'Very truly I tell you...' it's always to grab our attention to a major point.

Jesus' audience would have known that this was a quote from Genesis, the first book of the Bible: *'...he saw a stairway resting on the earth, with its top reaching to heaven, and the angels of God were ascending and descending on it.'* (Genesis 28:12)

So what is Jesus saying about Himself?

- Jesus is the way to heaven!
- He bridges the gap between God and humanity.
- He is God's long-promised Messiah, He brings God's presence to earth.

Come and see! The invitation to us is the same 2,000 years later.

Summary

People start following Jesus and they are amazed at who He is!

- John the Baptist is back, pointing to Jesus as the Lamb of God. (v. 36)
- Two of John's followers immediately know that the time is right to start following Jesus. (v. 37)
- Even just a day with Jesus is life-changing for these men. Invited to 'come and see,' they're certain they've found the long-promised Messiah. (v. 41)
- They just can't keep it to themselves. Andrew tells his brother, Simon (Peter). (v. 42)
- And Philip gives the same invite to Nathanael: 'Come and see.' (v. 46)
- Nathanael needs convincing, but after a one to one with Jesus he knows that Jesus is the Son of God, the King. (v. 49)
- And Jesus is only just getting started. He makes a radical claim, that He's the bridge between God and humanity, the way to heaven itself. (v. 51)

[36] 'Look, the Lamb of God!'

[37] ...they followed Jesus...

[41] 'We have found the Messiah.'

[42] And he brought him to Jesus.

[46] 'Come and see.'

[49] '...you are the Son of God; you are the king of Israel.'

[51] '...you will see "heaven open, and the angels of God ascending and descending on" the Son of Man.'

Why not find a moment to re-read what we've looked at in this episode?

John 1:35–51

[35] The next day John was there again with two of his disciples. [36] When he saw Jesus passing by, he said, 'Look, the Lamb of God!' [37] When the two disciples heard him say this, they followed Jesus. [38] Turning round, Jesus saw them following and asked, 'What do you want?' They said, 'Rabbi' (which means 'Teacher'), 'where are you staying?' [39] 'Come,' he replied, 'and you will see.' So they went and saw where he was staying, and they spent that day with him. It was about four in the afternoon. [40] Andrew, Simon Peter's brother, was one of the two who heard what John had said and who had followed Jesus.

[41] The first thing Andrew did was to find his brother Simon and tell him, 'We have found the Messiah' (that is, the Christ). [42] And he brought him to Jesus. Jesus looked at him and said, 'You are Simon son of John. You will be called Cephas' (which, when translated, is Peter). [43] The next day Jesus decided to leave for Galilee. Finding Philip, he said to him, 'Follow me.' [44] Philip, like Andrew and Peter, was from the town of Bethsaida. [45] Philip found Nathanael and told him, 'We have found the one Moses wrote about in the Law, and about whom the prophets also wrote – Jesus of Nazareth, the son of Joseph.' [46] 'Nazareth! Can anything good come from there?' Nathanael asked. 'Come and see,' said Philip. [47] When Jesus saw Nathanael approaching, he said of him, 'Here truly is an Israelite in whom there is no deceit.' [48] 'How do you know me?' Nathanael asked. Jesus answered, 'I saw you while you were still under the fig-tree before Philip called you.' [49] Then Nathanael declared, 'Rabbi, you are the Son of God; you are the king of Israel.' [50] Jesus said, 'You believe because I told you I saw you under the fig-tree. You will see greater things than that.' [51] He then added, 'Very truly I tell you, you will see "heaven open, and the angels of God ascending and descending on" the Son of Man.'

What comes next?
Jesus shows His glory in a surprising way... or was it?

Chapter 1: recap

Chapter 1 has invited us to take a close look at Jesus:

- **Episode 1:** John (the writer) says he is introducing us to God come to earth, Jesus Christ, who offers adoption for eternity into God's family.
- **Episode 2:** John the Baptist says Jesus fulfils the age-old prophecies. He has come to die, to pay the price we can't pay, to bring us back to God.
- **Episode 3:** Jesus immediately begins to gather followers. They are convinced He is the Messiah.

It's all about Jesus. It's not about the church or traditions. Jesus is:

- **The Word**: the Creator God become a man.
- **The Messiah**: long-promised as God's chosen ruler.
- **The Lamb of God:** come to die as a sacrifice for our sin.
- **The Spirit-filled Son:** bringing God's presence into our lives.
- **The gateway to heaven!**

What does this mean for us?

- The promise of John 1:12 is now possible through Jesus.

↓

'Yet to all who did receive him, to those who believed in his name, he gave the right to become children of God.'

'Come and see'

We hope you've enjoyed chatting through the first chapter of John's Gospel.

Keep reading to see more of Jesus through John's eyes, as Jesus' public life begins and His life-changing impact on those who were there unfolds.

You can get the next book at theword121.com.